D1443090

E
Is for
Environment

Also by Ian James Corlett

E Is for Ethics:
How to Talk to Kids about Morals, Values,
and What Matters Most

E
Is for
Environment

Stories to Help Children Care for Their World— at Home, at School, and at Play

Ian James Corlett

Illustrated by R. A. Holt

ATRIA BOOKS

New York   London   Toronto   Sydney

ATRIA BOOKS

A Division of Simon & Schuster, Inc.
1230 Avenue of the Americas
New York, NY 10020

First Atria Books hardcover edition February 2011

ATRIA BOOKS and colophon are trademarks of Simon & Schuster, Inc.

For information about special discounts for bulk purchases,
please contact Simon & Schuster Special Sales at 1-866-506-1949 or
business@simonandschuster.com.

The Simon & Schuster Speakers Bureau can bring authors to your
live event. For more information or to book an event, contact the
Simon & Schuster Speakers Bureau at 1-866-248-3049
or visit our website at www.simonspeakers.com.

Designed by Nancy Singer

Manufactured in China

10   9   8   7   6   5   4   3   2   1

Library of Congress Control Number: 2010025854

ISBN 978-1-4391-9455-3
ISBN 978-1-4391-9457-7 (ebook)

To all the kids who make me smile

"If many little people in many little places do many little deeds, they can change the face of the earth."
AFRICAN PROVERB

Contents

Foreword

Full disclosure. I've never been a tree hugger, a vegetarian, or even much of a gardener. In fact, I'm not a huge fan of the outdoors much at all. I like my fast sports cars, big cities, and, till recently, nearly any form of disposable thing. But like so many millions of others, I've started to become very aware of our environment and what we can do for it.

In the past few years, several events in particular made me sit up and take notice.

I began working on a TV project with some guys who were a bit younger than me. Their way of looking at the world was different. They pedaled up on their bikes to nearly every meeting. They carried reusable grocery bags long before that was hip. Or legislated! They spoke freely about conserving almost everything.

Then, one day in 2007, a colleague named Matt Hill pulled me aside to let me in on a very big secret. He was giddy and giggling as he whispered, "Steph [his girlfriend] and I are going to run around the whole of North America and raise a million bucks for the planet!"

Well, knowing that crazy Matty was prone to outright fabrication just to get a reaction, I immediately dismissed this with, "Yeah, and I'm having lunch with Donald Trump."

After a long pause and a steely stare, I realized he was being as serious as I had ever seen him. I felt a sudden rush of emotion filled with envy, pride, and more than a dash of guilt. I told him then and there that I would help out in any way I could.

A year later, he and Steph began running "a marathon a day" as they started their quest around the perimeter of North America. Supported by a biodiesel-fueled RV and not much else, the Run for One Planet movement had begun (www .runforoneplanet.com). They were really doing something.

After a full year on the road, they returned triumphant. It was more than reaching their million-dollar goal; they were triumphant in another way. During their journey, they quickly learned that there was another goal that might just turn out to be of even more value: teaching kids about the environment.

Along the way on their expedition, they brought their environmental message to tens of thousands of kids in hundreds of elementary schools. When they returned, I sensed an almost magical air about them. They had done something very important. And I knew it. And once again, I felt guilty. Yay, me!

Sometimes guilt is good. For me, anyway. It motivates me. It made me decide to convert my classic 1962 blue-smoke-belching Vespa scooter into a fully electric version. And I love it. Now I have all the head-turning fun of a multimirrored mod-style vintage Vespa with the conscience-soothing, completely silent, clean, and nonpolluting practicality of a thoroughly modern electric scooter. And I didn't stop there. Being a bit of a Porsche fanatic, I have also taken on an electro-conversion project on a 1966 Porsche. Nothing like zooming around town in a whisper-quiet classic sports car.

I started to think about what else I could do. And I realized I could put my P.O.D. (Plain Old Dad) credentials to work and decided to write this book full of fun stories featuring our favorite brother and sister, Elliott and Lucy, helping to spark discussion about making the planet a little better.

Ian

Introduction

Enviro-Warriors Matt and Steph Invade the School!

It was the first week of school, and there was excitement in the air. Matt and Steph, a couple of green crusaders, were visiting the school today. They were running more than 11,000 miles around the whole continent and were stopping at schools along their route.

In the gym, Elliott was sitting with his pals, and Lucy was sitting with hers. Matt and Steph arrived to talk about their run and how it was to raise awareness for the environment and help kids to take what they called "the environmental action challenge." They were both very enthusiastic.

Steph was really smart and knew everything about the environment, and Matt made everyone laugh with his silly voices and stories. Together, they talked about some of the crazy things that happened along their run, such as meeting UFO hunters and dealing with Matt's blistery feet, but most of all, they spoke about things kids can do every day to make the world a greener place—things like recycling, turning off lights, even how and what you eat.

They said it was as simple as three words: reduce, reuse, and recycle.

The coolest thing happened at the end of their presentation. They played this old song from their parents' generation called "Teach Your Children," which is all about teaching kids how to grow up to be good people. But when Matt and Steph said a super-secret word, all the grown-ups in the gym magically "disappeared" so they could share a tip just for kids. (The secret word was "rhubarb," and Matt *said* the grown-ups disappeared, but everyone could still see them.) That's when Matt told the kids that the real lyrics to the song should be, "*Kids,* teach your teachers *and* your parents well-*er.*" In "Matt-speak," there is "well" and "well*er*" along with "good" and "good*er.*"

So that meant that even though the teachers and all the parents were doing a great job teaching kids most things, *kids* can take the lead to help teach grown-ups ways to help the environment.

The presentation ended with a big cheer and a pinky-promise commitment from all the kids to take action to help the planet. Elliott and Lucy were especially enthused about it and decided to start taking action *right away.*

1

❧

It's in the Bag

Today it was Dad's turn to shop for groceries for dinner, so he took Elliott and Lucy with him to Wholesome Choices Market, the kids' favorite grocery store. Lucy loved going there to see all the beautiful displays of fresh fruit, vegetables, and flowers that came from farmers nearby.

Elliott liked to go to the grocery store because they always had creepy-looking fish on ice in the fish department. Elliott pretended that the fish were talking to one another, and he made up funny voices for them to match their mouths. "Hello, Mr. Salmon, how are things upstream today?" he would say. "Just fine, thank you, Mr. Trout," he'd reply in a deep voice. Lucy thought everything about fish was icky even if they did have funny voices. Dad agreed. He said he had a hard time eating things with a face on them. And those fish sure did have faces. Weird ones!

With that, Dad gave the kids jobs. He said it was like a treasure hunt for ingredients. "Lucy, you go find a package of spaghetti and also a jar of sauce called marinara. And be sure to get the one that says 'organic' on the package. Do you remember how to spell that?"

Lucy smiled and said, "Yup, and I know what it means, too: it's made without the yucky stuff!"

Dad just smiled and turned to Elliott. "Elliott, I want you to go get the lettuce, and along with making sure it says 'organic,' I want to see if you can get some that is local. All right?"

"Check!" Elliott replied.

Dad also asked him to get a cucumber and some carrots, too. Elliott complained that he had more things to get than Lucy, but Dad reminded him that his sister was smaller and this evened out the contest. "See you at the checkout. First one there wins . . . oh, and *no running*!"

They were off like a shot, and in record time they both came sliding to meet Dad at the front. "It's a tie!" Dad said with relief.

The kids caught their breath as Dad finished up with the cashier. "Would you like bags today, sir?" she asked. Just as Dad was about to answer "Yes," Lucy jumped in and said, "Dad, wait!"

QUESTION

Why do you think Lucy stopped her dad before he
could answer the question?

Dad didn't realize it, but Lucy had thought ahead and brought three reusable grocery bags from home. Whenever Mom went shopping, she always brought her own reusable bags, and this had now become a habit for Lucy, too. She answered because she knew her dad didn't have any with him that day. Bringing her own shopping bags meant that fewer paper bags needed to be used, saving energy and trees.

MORE QUESTIONS

◉ By using her own bag from home, did Lucy *reduce, reuse,* or *recycle*?
◉ Can you make a decision to remember to use a reusable bag when you go shopping?
◉ What other things in this story are healthy for the environment?

Depending on what it is made from, a plastic shopping bag can take anywhere from 15 to 1,000 years to decompose. In a compressed landfill, deprived of atmosphere to help them biodegrade, paper bags don't fare much better. Not only that, but many plastic bags find their way into our oceans and get eaten by turtles, birds, and other ocean dwellers. This can kill them.

"Great things are done by a series of small things brought together."
VINCENT VAN GOGH

2

ꝏ

A Mile a Day Keeps You
Feeling Okay

It was a beautiful Saturday morning with so much going on. There were soccer games to play, songs to practice on the piano, and even a little homework to finish. Lucy always loved the weekends, especially when there was a family project. And this weekend was going to be extra fun, because Mom planned to send out Elliott and Lucy's school photos to all of their friends and relatives.

Mom set up a little assembly line, with Elliott and Lucy writing the date, what grade they were in, and their ages on the backs of their photos. While they were doing this, Mom would write a card, address the envelope, and put the photos inside it. Then she would hand it all to Dad to seal up and put a postage stamp on. It was fun!

Elliott and Lucy made up a little song as they did their parts:

"First you lick, lick, lick, then you stick, stick, stick!" Elliott and Lucy thought their song was pretty good. So did Mom and Dad. Mom said they sounded like real rappers. This made the children smile. Soon they were done, and they had a nice, neat stack.

Elliott and Lucy were ready to run out the door and pop the photos into the mailbox at the end of their block, but Mom reminded them that the mail only got picked up twice a week from there. She wanted to make sure that their relatives far away received their photos soon, so she decided they should take them straight to the post office.

A trip to the post office sounded like fun to Elliott and Lucy. As Dad searched for his car keys, they remembered something that Matt and Steph had said about trips less than a mile. Elliott asked, "Dad, is the post office more than a mile away?" Dad replied that he thought it might even be *less* than a mile away. "Hmmm," Elliott thought, "less than a mile, and it's a sunny day . . ." His eyes brightened as he proclaimed, "Dad, put your keys away. I have an idea!"

QUESTION

What do you think Elliott's idea was?

One great way to save energy, pollute less, and be good to your body is to *expend* your energy. Elliott remembered Matt and Steph's suggestion, "If it's less than a mile, walk it with a smile!" The trip to the post office was a perfect chance to try it out. Mom and Dad agreed completely, and they really enjoyed the walk there and back. Try it yourself. A trip to the grocery store? The coffee house? The bookstore? If it's less than a mile, wherever you're going, try leaving the car at home.

MORE QUESTIONS

◉ How did the family help the planet by deciding to walk to the post office?

◉ What places can you walk to from where you live?

◉ Why is walking instead of driving good for the environment *and* for you?

Did you know that for every mile you drive, a pound to a pound and a half (if you drive an SUV) of carbon dioxide (air pollution or CO_2) pumps into the air? That's a lot of Yukk!

"Of all exercises walking is the best."
THOMAS JEFFERSON

"Anywhere is walking distance, if you have the time."
STEVEN WRIGHT

3

❧

Heat It or Beat It?

It was a blustery day outside, so any playtime would be indoors today. Elliott and Lucy headed to the playroom, which was right beside where Mom did the laundry. A neatly stacked pile of Elliott and Lucy's sweaters had to be moved to make some room to play. "We'll take these up to our rooms after we're finished," Elliott suggested. Lucy thought that was a great idea, too. Mom would be impressed.

Now that they had some room, they dove into building with their generic Danish building-block sets. Every time Elliott and Lucy built blocks together, they would decide on a theme. Sometimes it was robots, or airplanes, or trains, or even cars. But today's theme was city. City had a little of all of those. Lucy built houses. Elliott built schools and skyscrapers . . . oh, and robots. Robots go with everything, according to Elliott.

As Lucy was busy designing a tiny little fireplace, she looked outside and saw that it was beginning to rain. Rain always made Lucy feel chilly. Meanwhile, Elliott was busy building a sky-scraper, complete with air-conditioning units on top of it. As Elliott thought about air conditioners, he began to feel a little chilly, too. Neither he nor Lucy mentioned feeling chilly, so they just kept building. They weren't too cold . . . yet.

An hour passed, and while Elliott was busy making crazy-looking robots that would attack the city, Lucy had moved on to building cars for all of the houses she assembled. She looked a little troubled as she sat in front of a pile of red blocks. Finally, she asked, "What shape is a hybrid car?"

Elliott replied, "Well, a lot of them have a kind of funny shape, but hybrids come in all sorts of regular shapes of cars *and* trucks, too."

"Trucks? Super!" Lucy said. Those were the easiest to build. As she turned her attention back to building, she said, "Look, Elliott!" Outside the window, she noticed that the rain had turned to *snow*! Almost at the same time, the kids looked at each other and said, "That's why it feels so cold today!"

"I know what to do," Lucy said as she hopped up, walked past the couch with the sweaters on it, and headed toward the thermostat.

"Wait!" Elliott said. "I have a better idea!"

QUESTION

What "better idea" do you think Elliott had in mind to warm up?

10

Elliott realized that it wasn't super-duper freezing cold, so they didn't need to turn up the heat, they just needed to put on their sweaters. That was something that Matt and Steph had reminded the children at school. Why heat a whole house when you can just heat up yourself? That's what Elliott and Lucy decided. They put on some slippers, too, because keeping your tootsies warm makes all of you feel toasty.

MORE QUESTIONS

⑨ How does keeping the heat down help our environment?

⑨ Do you have one room where you live that is always a little chillier than the rest?

⑨ Have you ever built your own robot?

By keeping the heat low and putting on a sweater, you can save 1,000 pounds of carbon dioxide from the atmosphere per year.

If your tootsies are cold, your body will likely feel cold, too. Try placing area rugs on cold floors, and you'll be less likely to turn up the thermostat.

Ideas for room temperatures:
Sitting, reading, or watching TV: 70°F (21°C).
Working around the house: 68°F (20°C).
Sleeping: 61°F (16°C).
No one is home: 61°F (16°C).

4

The Hunt for Red Dots All Over

Lucy was looking very sneaky as she rummaged through her drawers to find black leotards, a black turtleneck, and black gloves. She pulled on each piece of clothing very carefully. She was almost completely dressed in black. Just one more piece, and her outfit would be complete.

She ran to the front closet where Mom kept the snow suits, gloves, and ski clothes. Aha! She found it. Elliott's black ski mask! She pulled it over her head, struck a pose, and announced, "Energy Vampire Hunter has arrived!"

Mom was watching all of this from the kitchen. As usual, she waited patiently to see just what Lucy was up to . . .

Lucy grabbed a clipboard, some scrap paper, and a pencil. Her eyes darted back and forth. "The hunt is on!" She started in the living room. She sneaked over to the TV, ninja-style. The TV was off, but she saw a red light glowing on it and marked something on the paper. She looked below it to the DVD player and the video game system. Hmm . . . more glowing red lights. She made some more marks, then scurried off to the family room beside the kitchen. Aha!

Dad had taken his computer to work, but the power adapter was still plugged into the wall. Energy Vampire Hunter spotted yet another glowing red dot on the little box on the computer cable. She made another mark on the paper. Then she saw Mom and Dad's cell-phone chargers, both plugged into the wall with no cell phones charging. Her pencil was scribbling madly now.

Lucy rushed upstairs and continued her hunt. When she raced back down to the kitchen, she presented Mom with her clipboard. "Mom? Energy Vampire Hunter formally requests permission to deal with this list of energy suckers!"

Mom carefully read the list and circled a couple of items. "I see . . . well, you can deal with all of these except the TV recorder, the telephone answering machine, and the microwave. They all have clocks or timers, so they need to stay plugged in."

Lucy jumped for joy with a mighty "Mission accomplished!"

QUESTION

What do you think Lucy the Energy Vampire Hunter asked
Mom for permission to do?

Lucy remembered from Matt and Steph's "action list" that there are many things in the house that keep using energy even if they are not being used. They are called Energy Vampires. They still keep using energy even if they are not turned on. Usually, it's called "standby" mode.

MORE QUESTIONS

- Why is it important to do more than simply turn off the power switch on some gadgets?
- Why was it good that Lucy ask her mom for permission before unplugging anything?
- Can you see anything in the room you're in right now that is in standby mode that your parents can unplug or turn off completely?

Studies estimate that standby power consumption in the United States accounts for 5 percent of all residential power consumption. That means Americans spend more than $3.5 billion annually on wasted power.

"Conservation means the wise use of the earth and its resources for the lasting good of men."
GIFFORD PINCHOT,
FIRST CHIEF OF THE U.S. FOREST SERVICE

5

Lola's "Business"

Having a pet pooch was fun. Elliott and Lucy loved to play fetch with Lola. They cuddled her and gave her lots and lots of love. Lola gave the love right back, especially after her morning walk. That's when Lola would do her "you know what," as Lucy called it. Mom called it "poopsies," Elliott called it "doo-doo," and Dad? Well, Dad just said, "she did her business."

When it was time for Lola to go potty, whoever took her outside needed to pick up after she "did her business." It's only polite. No one would appreciate a nice stroll in the park only to step in one of Lola's or some other doggie's "doo-doos." For the longest time, the family used a plastic grocery bag to clean up after Lola. But since they had started using reusable grocery bags, they didn't have as many around the house anymore. This was a problem.

Today was Elliott's turn for Lola's walk. He frantically searched high and low for some sort of bag to pick up her poop. Finally, he found one of Dad's old paper bags that he used to pack his lunch in. Elliott noticed that the bag had "biodegradable" written on it. Elliott knew that meant the bag was designed to fall apart and turn back to dirt easily. Perfect!

Elliott and Lola hurried to the park, and before you could say "plop, plop," Lola was done. Elliott quickly picked it up with the paper bag and dropped it into the park garbage can.

When Elliott got home, he declared to Mom that they needed a more permanent Lola bag solution. They sat down at the computer and went to their favorite online pet store. They found all sorts of poop bags, but Elliott was particularly drawn to a little container shaped like a cute doggie bone that clipped onto a leash that also held a nice little roll of doo-doo bags. "Great!" Mom said.

They clicked on that, put it in the online cart, and then looked at the bags that fit into it. There were two types of bags. Regular bright blue plastic ones and another type that looked just like regular black plastic roll bags but said "Made from Corn" on them. Hmm . . . The regular plastic bags were a lot cheaper, but those black bags were 100 percent biodegradable.

QUESTION

What kind of poopie bag do you think Elliott and his mom chose?

Elliott knew that when something was biodegradable, it was a better solution for the environment. Being biodegradable meant that the bags would break down or fall apart easily. He also knew that poop from a pooch, a kitty, a horse, or even a person was good for the earth. The nice word people use is "fertilizer," and it helps plants grow healthy and strong. Mom even suggested that they could put the poop into something called a composter in the yard, which is a container you can put food scraps, grass, leaves, and even doggie doo into to turn it into fresh, new, and healthy dirt for the garden. So it was pretty clear that Elliott and his mom chose the black biodegradable bags that were made out of corn.

MORE QUESTIONS

◉ Do you have a pooch? If so, do you pick up after it every time?
◉ Why does the type of bag you use for doggie doo-doo matter?

Dogs on average poop 23 times a week. That's an average of 15 to 30 pounds of waste per dog per year.

In a city of 100,000 people, dogs can generate about 2.5 tons of poop per day. That's almost 2 million pounds a year!

"Dachshunds, the only dog that's shaped like its own poop!"
TRIUMPH THE INSULT COMIC DOG
PUPPET DOG FROM *LATE NIGHT WITH CONAN O'BRIEN*

6

Look at Life from Both Sides Now

Lucy was very creative. She loved to write. She wrote notes. She wrote poems. She even wrote jokes. Like "What did the teddy bear say when he was offered dessert? Not for me, please, I'm stuffed!" She also colored and drew. She even made paper airplanes. And she was fast. She hopped from one piece of paper to another like a bee on fresh flowers. No sooner had she scribbled out a drawing of a horse than she switched gears and was designing a skyscraper. The same went for her notes. Just as soon as she had created a poem for Auntie Shannon, she whipped off an *I Love You* note to Mom or Dad.

All of this creativity used up a lot of materials. Lucy went through pencils and crayons like a beaver through a tree. When she stopped to think about it, she wondered if she was being just a teensy-weensy bit wasteful. And she was, kind of. She would often throw out a pencil, or crayon once it got a little stubby. She knew she could do better, but how?

Her first decision was about pencils. She decided then and there that each pencil she used would get sharpened and used until her little fingers couldn't grip it any longer. And the same went for crayons. Even if they broke in two, she vowed to keep both halves and use them till she couldn't hold on to them anymore.

Mom noticed that she didn't have to go to the office-supply store as often. This made Lucy very happy. She knew she was doing the right thing by not throwing away her supplies before she really had to.

But something else was bothering Lucy. When she looked at the stacks and stacks of paper that her creations were created with, she started to think. "Hmm . . . How many of these papers actually leave my room as gifts or notes?" In fact, not many of them at all ended up being given away or displayed. Lucy reasoned, "Mostly what I do is for practice. And I've only been using one side of the paper, just one side . . ." pondered Lucy.

QUESTION

What do you think Lucy is planning to do regarding her paper usage?

Lucy decided that while she was practicing and just being "creative," she would use both sides of the paper instead of only one. This way, she would cut her paper usage in half. When it came to making a good copy of a project, then and only then she could use a nice, fresh piece. Cutting down on paper waste is good for our environment. Don't forget, paper comes from trees.

MORE QUESTIONS

- Besides deciding to use less paper, how else did Lucy conserve or make better use of her materials?
- How can you use less when you're making projects?

Recycled or paper made from "postconsumer" waste paper is readily available and doesn't use any new trees at all.

Try to use unbleached or chlorine-free paper. Fewer chemicals mean less harm to us and our environment.

"Computers may save time but they sure waste a lot of paper. About 98 percent of everything printed out by a computer is garbage that no one ever reads."
ANDY ROONEY

"Every child is an artist. The problem is how to remain an artist once we grow up."
PABLO PICASSO

7

❧

Dental Arithmetic

One of Elliott's best subjects at school was math. He could add, subtract, divide, and multiply almost as easily as walking. Elliott loved to count how many trees they would pass on a walk around the park, then multiply or divide the number of trees just for fun. "For fun?" Dad would say as he scratched his head. Math didn't come so naturally for him.

So it made a lot of sense that Elliott would be playing math games as the members of the family were brushing their teeth one morning. Lucy was meticulous about brushing her teeth and made sure each one of them got special attention. After finishing each tooth on the top, she would spit, put her brush back under the water, which was still running, then continue with her bottom teeth. All the while, Elliott was taking notes, scribbling numbers, and timing her. When Elliott had finished observing Lucy, he watched Mom and Dad brush, too. He noticed that they all did the same thing. Everyone in the family, including himself, left the water running the whole time they brushed their teeth.

This got Elliott thinking. He wondered how much water was just going down the drain in the "in between" time when people were brushing their teeth. He went to some of the Web sites that Matt and Steph visit to learn about saving water. He learned that just turning off the faucet while brushing your teeth saves 10 quarts (or about 10 liters) of water each and every time.

Elliott's mind went into math mode, and he quickly started calculating. There were four people in their family who brushed their teeth twice a day, so that added up to 80 quarts of water that was wasted *every day*. He did another calculation and estimated that if they all kept the water running during brushing for their whole lives, as a family, they would waste more than 2 million quarts of water!

Elliott resolved to take action, and that night at dinner, he politely asked, "Dad? May I suggest a new family rule?"

"Probably," Dad replied, "but before you do, whisper it in my ear." Elliott whispered his idea, and Dad nodded his head yes. "Go ahead, Elliott, that sounds like a good family rule."

QUESTION

What do you think Elliott's new idea for a family rule was?

You guessed it. Elliott suggested that the new family rule was to turn off the water while brushing your teeth. They all agreed that it was a good idea. And then they thought about how they were going to do it. Sure, it seemed a little weird at first, but it was just a habit to leave the water running. Old habits can be replaced with new ones, and it makes it even easier to adjust to a new habit if you know it's a good one.

MORE QUESTIONS

◉ Do you leave the water running as you brush your teeth?
◉ Do you think your teeth are any cleaner by letting the water run as you brush?

All waste water (the water that goes down the drain) gets "treated" or cleaned up by your city or town's water system. That treatment uses energy and costs money. So the less water down the drain, the better.

"A little water is a sea to an ant."
AFGHAN PROVERB

8

⚬◦⚬

Litterless Lunch

Elliott and Lucy always helped Mom pack their lunches for school. Lucy's favorite part of making her lunch was picking out her recess snack. She would close her eyes and rummage around the bottom pantry shelf till her fingers felt the right "magical vibe" to pull out just the right treat. There were tiny packages of organic roll-ups, gummies, healthy fish-shaped crackers, and raisins. Even though she liked them all, sometimes her "magic" would make a mistake, and she'd toss the snack back and pick a new one. Hey, that's what made Lucy Lucy! Elliott, on the other hand, liked gummies on Mondays, crackers on Tuesdays, raisins on Wednesdays, and . . . well, he liked routine.

But today was different. Lucy opened the pantry and was shocked. Instead of a shelf full of little packages, there were just large bags in their place. One was full of gummies and another with fish-shaped crackers but no little packages. "Mom? What are we supposed to do with this?" Lucy wondered.

"I was thinking that we make a lot of garbage every week just from the packaging of your little snacks," Mom said. "It's time to cut back and save the garbage cans from getting filled up with snack wrappers."

Both Elliott and Lucy thought this was a good idea, since they had been learning about landfills and throwing less stuff out.

Mom showed them reusable containers she had bought that were made exactly the right size for their sandwiches. "I thought we should try to make a litterless lunch," Mom said. She explained that "litterless" meant having no wrapping or packaging that had to be thrown in the garbage. Everything should be reusable.

"Good thinking, Mom!" Elliott said.

"And we already use these," said Lucy, plopping their reusable water bottles and veggie containers onto the counter. "But what are we going to do about the snacktime snacks?"

Mom replied, "I'm going to let you think that one out, kids." She smiled and pointed to the other counter, which had on it sheets of wax paper, plastic sandwich bags, tiny paper bags, and some brand-new small reusable containers with lids.

QUESTION

Which item will complete the kids' litterless lunch?

It didn't take Elliott and Lucy long to decide which item would be truly litterless for their snacks. Since they were already using reusable containers for their vegetables and the new ones Mom just got for their sandwiches, the choice was clear. They picked the new small reusable snack-sized containers. And the kids' lunches were just the beginning. Lucy suggested that Dad should try the litterless lunch idea, too.

MORE QUESTIONS

◉ Do you think you could try to make a litterless lunch?
◉ Even though the reusable containers are a great idea, what must you remember to do with them after they're used each time?

Close to 2.7 billion juice boxes end up in landfills every year.

Each child who brings a brown-bag lunch to school every day will generate 67 pounds of waste by the end of the school year. That's 18,760 pounds of lunch waste for an average-sized school.

Lunchtime trash is second only to office paper as the leading source of school waste.

"Unless someone like you cares a whole awful lot, nothing is going to get better. It's not."
DR. SEUSS

9

∽∾

Stuffed Stuff and More Stuff

Every week, despite Mom and Dad's reminders, Elliott and Lucy's rooms got dirty. Well, not *dirty* but messy, especially Elliott's room. He said it was because he had a lot of things on his mind, such as the kind of spaceship he'd build if the Galaxy Fleet appointed him chief designer. He knew that wasn't an excuse for having a messy room . . . mostly because Dad said it wasn't! So, once a year, the whole family had a big spring cleaning. For the kids, this meant going through all of their toys and "stuff" and getting rid of anything they didn't use anymore. And that meant that a local charity would receive several big boxes of toys.

This was a difficult task for a collector like Elliott. He collected all sorts of trading cards, building-block sets, books, and comics. Giving up stuff was difficult for him. Every time he pulled out a toy, a book, or a piece of clothing, he would hold it in his hand

and remember all the good times he'd had with it. Like his old stuffed bunny Fluffy. "Oh, Fluffy. I remember when we used to snuggle in our car on trips. Those were good times . . ."

Elliott went through everything one at a time and started to notice a pattern. He had so many things that were very similar. He didn't have just one stuffed bunny. He had four! Elliott remembered that he persuaded Dad to buy him a new one each time he went to the toy store, because there was always a newer, cooler, more special version of the stuffed bunny he already had. One was really just about the same as the other, but he never realized that when he was little. All he knew then was that he *had* to have the new one. Looking back now, it all seemed a bit silly to Elliott, and he said so.

"That is some very grown-up thinking you're doing, son." Dad agreed that it was very common to want the latest and greatest thing. Even he fell into that when he was looking for a camera or a car. "We all need to ask ourselves, do we really need it? It takes an awful lot of time, energy, and money to keep buying and buying and buying more and more stuff," Dad said.

Elliott looked at the huge pile of stuff he was about to give away and took a deep breath. He scanned the other stuff in his room and said, "Dad, I think I have a new plan for me not to have so much stuff in the first place."

QUESTION

What do you think Elliott's new plan was?

Elliott had decided to adopt Dad's idea of asking himself if he *really needed* something before he bought it. He knew that if he could cut down the amount of stuff he got, it would help the environment. Every item we buy is built using materials, is shipped using energy, and, in the end, is probably thrown out, filling up our garbage dumps. In Elliott's family's case, they were donating their old stuff to charity, reusing, or recycling it. And that's a good thing to do!

MORE QUESTIONS

☉ Is your room more like Elliott's or Lucy's?

☉ How much stuff do you have that you really don't need?

☉ Can you make a plan to recycle your old stuff to a charity?

Watch the "Story of Stuff" for a fun and educational look at why we have so much stuff! Look for it at www.storyofstuff.com.

The average U.S. person now consumes twice as much as he or she did 50 years ago.

> *"A house is just a place to keep your stuff while you go out and get more stuff."*
> GEORGE CARLIN

10

❧

Ooh-La-La . . . Local

Lucy was spending the day with Auntie Shannon. She loved her "Shanny days," as she called them. They sometimes consisted of a special bike ride, a "girly-girl spa day" in her groovy apartment, or Lucy's favorite, cooking. That's because cooking with Shannon was not just making mac and cheese. Nope, it was *gourmet* cooking, which meant spending a lot of time, care, and attention.

Today's cooking theme was "Ooh-la-la!" That meant that everything was going to have a French flair. Shannon had a list of the ingredients she needed, which she knew she could get at the local organic market. Even though it was a little chilly out, they hopped on their bikes, and off they went.

As they were riding, Lucy called out, "What's for dessert?"

"I have some homemade French vanilla ice cream and I thought I'd leave the fruit topping choice to you!" replied Shannon.

Lucy blurted out, "Mango!" Lucy remembered trying a mango at Shannon's in the summer and liking it.

"Okay, we'll find some mango!" This made Lucy happy.

The market was fun. It had foods that were local and organic. "I love buying local ingredients, just the way a fine chef would," said Shannon as they headed to the fruit stand.

The friendly fruit seller answered sadly, "I'm sorry, but mangos are only in summer. "And even then, we don't have them. Mangos don't grow anywhere near here. But hey, I have some super-sweet apples!"

Lucy looked kind of grumpy. Shannon could see that Lucy was disappointed. "I think we can get mangos at the super-mega-market. They bring in tropical fruits all year round there."

Lucy perked up and asked, "You mean, the mangos have to come off a plane or something from the other side of the world?" Shannon nodded, but Lucy looked even more troubled. She remembered that Matt and Steph had said to "eat locally" as much as possible, which meant eating things that were from nearby instead of eating food flown in from all over the world and wasting energy. She thought hard for a moment, turned back to the fruit seller, and asked, "Can I have a taste of those super-sweet apples you were talking about?" Shannon smiled.

QUESTION

What do you think Lucy decided, and why?

Lucy decided to eat locally. So she chose the apples, and Shannon made a lovely caramel-style apple topping for dessert that was super-yummy. Lucy felt good that she had made a decision that meant that fuel for boats or planes wasn't needed so they could enjoy a yummy dessert. Shannon was so impressed that she promised Lucy that whenever she was cooking, she'd do her best to use local ingredients, too.

MORE QUESTIONS

◎ Are there markets near you that sell things from local farms?
◎ Can you explain what it means to eat locally?

Some foods like mangos travel from where they are grown by airplane. Others come by boat, such as bananas. Airplane shipping is very expensive and far worse for our environment than a boatload of bananas. Enjoy your bananas!

The U.S.A. has lost more than 5 million farms since 1935. So, who is growing all the food we eat? Most of us picture a farm as a place with a friendly farmer in overalls chewing a piece of straw as he milks his cow. Nope. Mostly, we have giant farms that look more like factories now.

"Vegetables are a must on a diet. I suggest carrot cake, zucchini bread, and pumpkin pie."
JIM DAVIS

11

Charge It

Elliott loved his gadgets. Can you blame him? He had some great ones, such as his handheld video game, his camera, his music player . . . and that didn't include his toys. There was his battery-operated train that puffed out "real" steam, the electric helicopter, and Elliott's favorite, Randolph the Robot. Most of the toys ran on batteries, and Elliott needed to visit Mom's "battery bin" often. Today, right in the middle of blasting its way out of an imaginary robo-battle, poor Randolph slowed and slowed until he just . . . stopped. Batteries dead.

Elliott pulled out the four dead batteries and headed to the kitchen garbage can with Randolph tucked under his arm. Mom said, "Uh-uh. Batteries don't go in the regular garbage, Elliott. They go in the recycling bin." Elliott had forgotten that and immediately dropped the old batteries into the recycling area. Then he grabbed the box where Mom kept the new batteries.

As Elliott was searching for the right-size battery, he said, "I wish this guy used rechargeable batteries, then I could just plug him in, and in an hour or so, he'd be as powerful as ever!"

Mom agreed and reminded Elliott that using rechargeable batteries meant not throwing out so many dead ones. She also said she had heard that some rechargeable batteries had even more power and lasted longer than regular ones.

Elliott stopped immediately. "More power, huh?" he said with wide eyes. "Is there a rechargeable battery size for Randolph?" Mom nodded. Elliott continued, "You're sure that rechargeable ones have more power so Randolph might last longer in a battle?" Mom nodded again. Elliott then asked, "And what about for my video game? Do those super-powerful rechargeables come for that, too?" Again, Mom answered yes.

Elliott's lips curled into a wicked smile. "A more powerful robot sounds cool! And maybe more power for my video game would increase my high scores, too!"

Mom answered, "Well, I don't know about that, but it sure would reduce waste, Elliott."

That was all Elliott needed to hear. He puffed out his chest and asked, "Mom? How much do I have in my allowance? Enough to by some rechargeable batteries?" Elliott had a plan.

QUESTION

What do you think Elliott was planning to do?

Elliott had more than high scores and a longer-lasting Randolph the Robot on his mind. He knew that recycling of any kind was a good thing for the environment. When you reuse something, such as a rechargeable battery, it's a good idea. But the possibility of a super-powered bot was a pretty cool bonus.

MORE QUESTIONS

◉ Was Elliott about to reuse, reduce, or recycle in this story?

◉ How many toys or devices do you have that run on batteries?

Rechargeable batteries have up to 28 times less impact on
the environment than regular (alkaline) batteries.

Rechargeable batteries can be reused up to 1,000 times.

Rechargeable batteries consume up to 23 times
less natural resources.

*"I once bought my kids a set of batteries for Christmas
with a note on it saying, toys not included."*
BERNARD MANNING,
BRITISH COMEDIAN

12

∽

With Your Own Two Eyes (and Nostrils)

Lucy was a real "action taker." You'd often hear her repeating, "Be careful what you throw away, because it all ends up in land filth!" She was so enthusiastic. When Lucy decided she was going to take action for the environment, she wanted everyone else to do so as well.

Today, Mom was cutting up cardboard boxes to take to the recycling bin when Lucy said to her, "Mom, did you know all that cardboard will end up in land filth?"

Mom smiled. "Yes, I do know most garbage ends up in the dump, but those places are called 'landfills,' and they *are* filthy, so I understand why you mixed it up." This was embarrassing to Lucy, who realized she was using the wrong words. "But this cardboard is going to the recycling bin, not the garbage," said Mom as she finished cutting up the cardboard. "I have a great idea. I need to drop this off at the recycling center, so why not come with me and see what a real landfill or dump looks like?"

Lucy answered, "Sure!" This sounded like an adventure.

When they got to the dump, the first thing Lucy noticed was the awful, stinky, poopy, make-your-eyes-water smell of the place. "That stinky smell is actually kind of good, Lucy," Mom said. She explained that the smell meant that the garbage was rotting or turning back into dirt. But then Mom showed Lucy all of the plastic bottles that were mixed in with the stinky, rotting garbage. "Those plastic bottles won't rot at all," Mom said. "They'll be here for hundreds or even thousands of years." She also showed Lucy a bunch of old car tires, some TVs, and a pile of computers. Mom said that the tires could have been crunched up and made into other things, and the computers could be recycled, too, but in the dump, they'd just sit. For a long, long time. That wasn't good.

Lucy's eyes were very wide. Now she really understood what a garbage dump or landfill was. "Thanks for bringing me here today, Mom. Now I have even more reasons why we should recycle. And I'm going to make a new promise."

QUESTION

What promise do you think Lucy was going to make?

Lucy was going to make a promise to recycle everything she could. Recycling is a great way to give things that could be yucky to our environment a new use. Mom's cardboard will be chopped, crunched, and mushed up and made into paper. Plastic bottles can be crunched up and used as soft filling for pillows or warm coats. Lucy was going to try to keep her recycling promise by checking twice before throwing anything into the garbage. That meant Mom and Dad were going to have to get a bigger recycling bin!

MORE QUESTIONS

◉ What was Lucy trying to talk about when she used the word "land filth"?

◉ Why are garbage dumps stinky?

◉ Have you ever been to the dump?

Americans buy an estimated 29.8 billion
plastic water bottles every year.

Nearly eight out of every ten bottles will end up
in a garbage dump (landfill).

*"In California they don't throw their garbage away—
they make it into TV shows."*
WOODY ALLEN

13

Bottled Up

Elliott could hardly believe his ears when Lucy told him that the plastic water bottles at the landfill would be there for up to a thousand years before they disappeared or turned into dirt. Their family used to buy lots of water in bottles, handy little bottles, big bottles, and giant bottles. "Remember when Mom got the water filter installed in the sink?" he said. "That sure made my job easier!" Being a healthy family, they drank a lot of water, which meant that Elliott had to carry a lot of bottles to the recycling box.

Elliott remembered carriing out 14 bottles one day!"

But all of that ended when they got the little water filter put in. Now they just went to the sink with their glass or reusable bottle and filled it up as many times as they were thirsty. Lucy and Elliott felt pretty good that Mom was thinking ahead and they were not using any more disposable water bottles.

"There was a lot more than just plastic bottles at the dump," Lucy recalled. "There were TVs and computers and a mountain of tires!"

That made Elliott remember the time Dad took him to the tire shop when his tires were worn out. Dad told Elliott that the tire shop sent the old tires to a recycler that would turn the worn-out tires into shoes, sports fields, stuff to build houses out of, even roads. "Tires driving on old tires! Get it, Lucy? 'Cause some roads are made out of old . . . Lucy?"

But she was lost in thought, just staring at the fridge.

"Are you too hungry to laugh at my joke?" Elliott asked.

"No, Elliott. It's not that at all . . ."

Deep in thought, Lucy walked over to the fridge, opened the door, and looked in. She saw jars of jam, vegetables, a plate of cake, and then there were all the drinks. There were two big plastic milk jugs, an orange juice jug, and three other types of juices in jugs that looked very similar to the milk jug.

She called Elliott over to look. "When we were talking about all the plastic water bottles we used to put into recycling, it made me wonder if there were other plastic containers we should recycle."

Elliott saw all the jugs on the "reachable" shelf. He understood.

Lucy declared, "I know some other bottles we need to make sure we recycle."

QUESTION

What do you think Lucy was planning?

Lucy was going to make sure that *all* of the family's plastic bottles and containers ended up in the recycling bin. When she was at the dump, she was thinking only about water bottles because she saw so many of them, but there are a lot of other bottles we use every day that should be recycled.

MORE QUESTIONS

◉ Look in your fridge and count how many plastic bottles and containers there are. Can you promise to recycle those?
◉ What can old tires be made into?

Plastic is made from oil. It takes 24 million gallons of oil to produce 1 billion plastic bottles—that's a LOT!

Recycling a single plastic bottle can conserve enough energy to light a 60-watt light bulb for up to six hours.

"Listen up, you couch potatoes: each recycled beer can saves enough electricity to run a television for three hours."
DENIS HAYES,
COORDINATOR OF THE FIRST EARTH DAY

14

Sports Share

Elliott looked forward to his soccer games. He loved getting to-gether with the other guys on his team, the Strikers. He enjoyed practicing his fancy footwork with Terrence, defending with Michael, and trying to score on Wyatt. They were a good group and always had a good time. On the weekends, the games were at the park across from Elliott's house, and the rest of the time, they played on another field. Elliott called them "road trips" that he and Dad would drive to. Elliott enjoyed traveling to the games with Dad, because they could talk about guy stuff. You know, outer space, sports, cowboys, cars. Elliott enjoyed the "alone time" with just Dad. Dad did, too.

They got the schedule about a week ahead of time, and when it came in, Dad would check the map to see where the game was. This week, Dad realized that the game was a long way away.

Elliott asked, "How far is it?"

Dad checked the computer. "It's thirty miles there and back, Elliott," he said. "It's probably going to take about forty-five minutes to get there." Dad reminded Elliott to come armed with lots to talk about, since this would be a long trip. "We'll be able to talk and talk and talk," Dad said with a smile.

Elliott started to think of things that he and Dad could discuss on the journey. Then something occurred to him. He asked, "Remember the last time we were going to a game and you talked about our car's efficiency? What did that mean again?"

Dad explained that efficiency meant how far your car could go on a tank of gas. "And our old car is not that efficient, I'm afraid."

Elliott had more questions. "Dad? Does the car use more gas if there is more stuff in it?"

Dad said it *might* but not much.

"So we'd use almost the same amount of gas for just the two of us to get to the game or if the car was full of people?" Elliott asked.

Dad had a pretty good idea of what Elliott was thinking. "But what about our alone time?" Dad asked.

Elliott replied, "I think I can sacrifice a little you-and-me time for the sake of the planet, Dad." Elliott picked up the phone and started dialing with a big smile.

QUESTION

What do you think Elliott was going to do?

Even though Elliott really enjoyed his "Dad time," he was willing to share it with his friends if it meant that he could make a better decision for the environment. In this case, it meant that up to five of his friends could get to the game using almost the same energy, or unleaded gas, as just him and Dad. Elliott didn't realize it, but he was starting his soccer club's first carpool. Soon all of the parents were taking turns filling up their cars with parents and soccer players for every away game.

MORE QUESTIONS

◉ Can you think of activities you can share rides to?

◉ Why is using less gas good for the environment?

◉ What is a carpool lane? Do you get to use it often?

Carpools have many benefits. Fewer cars full of more people mean less air pollution, and that means clean air so we can live healthier lives. Oh, and jokes! A car full of people is a great place to laugh!

"There can be economy only where there is efficiency."
BENJAMIN DISRAELI

15

Green Gifts

It was springtime, and at school, Elliott and Lucy had just heard about something called National Family Month, which was the time between Mother's Day and Father's Day. This year, to mark the beginning of National Family Month, the kids decided to celebrate it with one special Mom *and* Dad weekend. Elliott had all sorts of ideas. He suggested a perfume for Mom that he had seen advertised on TV. The commercial showed a lady standing on a yacht, with her dress flowing in the wind as it blew her perfume all over the place. "The bottle is huge, Lucy. Mom will love it!" And for Dad, Elliott just knew he'd like the aftershave the sea captain splashes on in another commercial. "And that bottle with the sailing ship on it is even bigger! Dad could really splash that stuff on!"

Lucy wasn't so sure. She wanted to make gifts, like a clay pot to hold flowers for Mom or a picture frame made out of macaroni for Dad. Elliott reminded her that they had already done that last year. "You're right," said Lucy, and she mumbled, "Mom and Dad are always so busy, I wish we could just get them a gift of time!" She giggled, realizing that what she had just said sounded a bit silly.

"Stuff? Time?" Elliott said. "That's it, Lucy! If we get Mom and Dad more stuff, we're just making more things that might get thrown away. Or something that they might not ever use."

Lucy held her nose. "You mean your stinky perfume idea?"

Elliott laughed in agreement "Mom and Dad don't need more stuff." Lucy looked confused as Elliott continued, "We're going to plan a whole day of activities where we can spend *time* with Mom and Dad." Lucy was starting to understand now. Elliott was bursting with ideas. "We could start with pancakes and breakfast in bed. Then we could play board games, then go for a walk to Mom's favorite street where all the antiques stores are. Oh, and then we can pack a lunch and eat it together at the park and then finish it off with a bike ride!" Lucy could hardly keep up with his ideas, but she thought they were all pretty good! "Mom and Dad will love spending all that time together as a family," Elliott proclaimed. "And it's good for the environment. And us, too!"

QUESTION

How was Elliott's idea for family time good for their health and the environment?

Parents love spending time with their kids on special occasions. It is time spent together that creates memories, and, unlike a little gift, memories last a lifetime. Elliott's plan got everyone out of the house and active, which meant that they would be having fun and being healthy, too. Even though presents are nice, it's good to make sure that we're not just getting more stuff that will be quickly forgotten. Or eventually throw away. The gift of time is more valuable than almost anything. And that works for kids and adults.

MORE QUESTIONS

⊚ Why were Elliott's first gift ideas not so good?
⊚ What is the best present you've ever given your mom or dad?
⊚ What activities would your parents enjoy?

Ideas! If you really must buy a gift, how about
a ticket to a museum you can all go to?

Make homemade "time coupons" on paper for Mom and Dad:
GOOD FOR ONE NAP
GOOD FOR 15 MINUTES OF CUDDLING
GOOD FOR HALF AN HOUR OF "QUIET TIME"

"Time is the most precious thing you own."
PROVERB

16

Fair-weather Gardener

Ever since Elliott was little, he'd enjoyed digging, planting, and working in the yard and garden. He was a lot like his grandpa that way. Grandpa loved to come over and work in Elliott and Lucy's yard and garden, because since he and Grandma moved to their apartment, he didn't have a garden of his own anymore. When Grandpa would come over, Elliott was always there right beside him. Grandpa said that Elliott had a "green thumb." Elliott checked his thumb carefully but didn't notice any green on it. Grandpa explained, "That just means you're good with plants!" Elliott laughed, then smiled because he'd learned something new.

As a result, Elliott and his green thumb were put in charge of some yard chores. He loved it! He looked after picking the weeds in the walkway, and he happily removed the dead leaves from Dad's prized rosebushes. *Ouch!* But he had to be careful, rosebushes are full of prickles! Elliott was also in charge of watering the lawn. In Elliott and Lucy's town, there were rules for conserving, or not wasting water. So only on certain days was watering the lawn allowed.

One day, Elliott had finished dinner and was watching TV, waiting for the news to be over so he could watch his favorite cartoon, *Krazy Kartoon Kapers Starring Klink and Klank,* which came on right after. But first he had to sit through the weather forecast with Pete Sprinkles, the always-laughing weatherman.

"Well, folks, our beautiful weather is about to come to an end. You'd better get the umbrellas, because we're about to have three full days of rain!" said the silly weather guy as he opened up a gigantic umbrella and laughed and laughed.

"I think he's what Grandpa calls a nincompoop," Elliott said as he rolled his eyes and waited for it to be over.

Suddenly, Mom called from the other room, "Elliott, it's time to turn on the sprinkler to water the lawn!"

Elliott was about to jump up and do it when he stopped and thought about what Pete the weatherman had just said. He walked over to Mom and said, "Nope, Mom, I'm not going to water the lawn today."

Mom looked a little upset until Elliott explained why.

QUESTION

Why would Elliott refuse to water the lawn?

Even though Elliott really wanted to watch cartoons, he still paid attention to the giggling weatherman. Elliott knew it was about to rain for several days, so he did not need to turn the sprinkler on to water the lawn. Mother Nature would look after that by raining on it! That meant Elliott was doing his part to save water. Good going, Elliott!

MORE QUESTIONS

- What did Elliott enjoy doing with his grandpa?
- What does having a "green thumb" mean? Is that different from "being green"?
- Do you like working in the yard?

More than half of the residential water used in a typical Western city goes to outdoor landscape watering.

A good way to see if your lawn needs watering is to step on the grass with your tootsies. If it springs back up when you step away, it doesn't need water. If it stays flat, the lawn is ready for watering.

"If the grass is greener on the other side of the fence, you can bet the water bill is higher."
AUTHOR UNKNOWN

17

Veggie Night

When it was Dad's turn to cook, he always liked to try something new. Elliott and Lucy never knew what to expect when Dad put on the apron. He liked themes to his dinners. One night, his theme was "roughing it," and he served baked beans still in the can! He called it "Cowboy Eatin'," handed everyone a fork, and said, "Dig in."

Tonight, Dad decided it was going to be "Veggie Night." He was going to make veggie burgers and tofu weenies on the barbecue. He also had French fries, green beans, and two types of salads: crispy green lettuce salad and crunchy, creamy cole slaw. Yum! As Dad was barbecuing, he told the kids about something he'd just learned.

"You know most burgers come from cows, right?" They knew that. "Did you know that cows pollute the atmosphere more than cars do?" he said with a smile.

Elliott and Lucy shook their heads, and Mom smiled and said, "Sweetie, I don't think this is the right time to talk about this." Now the kids *really* wanted to hear all about it.

"Have you ever heard Grandpa say he has a little gas?"

Elliott giggled, "Sure, all the time! It means he's tooting!"

Everyone laughed, and Dad went on to explain that cows do a lot of tooting. And that produces a gas. That gas, called methane, floats up into the sky and creates problems for the earth. "In fact, cows produce more gas emissions than cars do!" said Dad. "Hard to believe, isn't it?" Elliott's and Lucy's eyes were very wide in amazement. "But this dinner isn't contributing to any of that problem at all! *No-Cow Vegetarian* dinner is served!"

Everyone jumped in to eat, and it was all really delicious. Between bites, Lucy whispered to Elliott. "So, according to Dad, by not eating meat, we can help the environment?"

Elliott responded, "Yup, it's true. But I like my roast beef and hamburgers too much! So I wouldn't want to stop eating meat altogether," he said. "But I could do it a little."

"Like once a week?" Lucy suggested.

Elliott thought about it, "Sure! Every little bit helps, right?"

Lucy nodded. She cleared her throat, smiled, stood up, and said, "Family? Elliott and I have a great idea for dinner once a week."

QUESTION

What do you think Lucy was about to suggest?

Lucy thought it would be a great idea to try to have a vegetarian meal once a week. She knew eating a vegetarian dinner didn't mean just cutting out the beef, it meant not eating anything with a face—such as pork, chicken, or fish. It was a good way to help the environment and eat healthy a little bit at a time. Not everyone will eat vegetarian-style all the time, but why not try it once a month or once a week? Even though Elliott can't live without his roast beef and burgers, he understood the impact that all of the tooting cows have on the planet!

MORE QUESTIONS

◉ Would you like to try some of Elliott and Lucy's dad's cooking?
◉ What is methane gas?
◉ Could you try one vegetarian meal a week in your home?

Rain forests are still being knocked down so cows that will be made into hamburger can graze. Eating vegetarian saves one acre of forest every year.

Farm animals are ranked second in causing global warming. Reason: methane gas from prolific tooting and burping . . . eeww!

"We all love animals. Why do we call some 'pets' and others 'dinner'?"
K.D. LANG

18

Banana Boy

Elliott loved bananas. And he loved that they were good for him, too! Since he was tiny, Mom said, Elliott's favorite treat was always a banana. Mom and Dad called him a little monkey because he always seemed to have a banana in his hand. He even did a school report on them (which gave him an excuse to enjoy his favorite fruit while he was doing his homework). Elliott learned all sorts of things about bananas. They contain vitamins and tasty sugars, and the word *banana* comes from an Arab-language word, *banan*, which means "finger." Oh, and Elliott's favorite: The world's longest banana split was made in Australia and was four and a half miles long!

Another fact Elliott knew about bananas was that they grow in tropical climates, which means that they come from a long way away. So when Lucy reminded him to try to "eat local," this was very tough for Elliott. Bananas were something he just couldn't give up. "I understand, Elliott," Lucy said. "It would be like someone asking me to have only one doll . . . it would be super-hard." Elliott was relieved. He just couldn't live without his bananas.

One day, Elliott and Mom were at the grocery store, and he headed straight to the fruit section to grab a fresh bunch of bananas. Hmm. There were two types of bananas there, bananas called "fair trade" and regular bananas. The regular ones were a tiny bit cheaper, so Elliott reached for a bunch of those, since Dad told him always to check the price before you buy something.

Mom stopped him and said, "Do you know what fair trade bananas are, Elliott?" Elliott was very interested as Mom explained that the fair trade bananas were a little more expensive because the farmers and workers who grew them were treated fairly and were able to provide for their families. She also said that a lot of fair trade farms worked much harder not to use as many chemicals to keep weeds away or grow the bananas quicker, so that meant it was good for the environment, too. Elliott's eyes lit up when he heard that.

QUESTION

Now that he knew what fair trade meant, which banana bunch do you think Elliott chose?

Part of being good to the environment means being good to people. The fair trade bananas were better for the workers growing the fruit, so it meant they were happy. Many fair trade growers are trying to find ways to use fewer chemicals in growing their crops, and that means that the bananas are healthier to eat, besides not polluting the environment.

MORE QUESTIONS

- ◉ What is your favorite fruit?
- ◉ Have you ever heard of other fair trade foods—like coffee, mangos, pineapples, and grapes?
- ◉ How would Elliott's decision that will make others happy?

The banana is the most popular fruit in the world
and is available year round.

The majority of banana plantation workers who do not
work on fair trade plantations don't even earn enough
to live and support their families.

"When you buy fair trade products you can guarantee that the farmers who have worked hard to grow them get a minimum price. Fair trade is a way of giving regular support—and enjoying delicious high-quality foods at the same time."
EMMA THOMPSON

19

Cold-water Blues

Mom and Dad were sitting at the dinner table one evening, and Dad was going through the household bills. He looked at the phone bill and said, "Wow."

He looked at the cable TV bill, sighed, and said, "Wow."

He looked at the heating bill and said, "Oh . . . super-wow!"

Lucy thought he was happy when he was saying "wow," so she hopped onto his lap and said, giggling, "What's super-wow, Dad?"

Dad smiled as he replied, "Well, Lucy-pie, I meant super-wow in sort of a bad way. Our heating bill is really high!"

Lucy's giggles stopped. "Oh. That's not the kind of "wow" I was thinking, either," she said. Lucy was a little sad now. She knew that "high" meant it cost a lot of money. "So you mean you have to pay to heat the house?" she asked innocently.

"Yup, and the water, too," Dad explained. "When water comes

into our house from the city pipes, it's cold, like the water you get out of the outside hose. But when you want hot water, we need to heat it up." Lucy thought he was talking about when Mom heated up the water on the stove for spaghetti. Dad smiled and said, "No, Lucy, I'm talking about the hot water we use for baths and showers and washing our hands."

Lucy stopped to think. "So you mean that every time we have a hot bath or a shower or wash our hands using the hot faucet, it costs money?" Lucy asked.

Dad answered, "Yes, and the reason it costs money is that it takes energy, and in our house it's electricity, to heat the water." Dad explained that it was electricity that cost the most money.

"And if we only used cold water to wash our hands and for baths, it would save you money and save electricity?" Lucy asked.

Dad laughed when he imagined the family having ice-cold baths or showers, but he did agree that washing hands in cold water would probably help.

Lucy remembered something else, too, "I've seen laundry soap that is made for cold water. Will the washing machines work with only cold water, too?" Dad nodded. Lucy's little mind was racing. She had a new "action" in mind that would save the family money and reduce the amount of electricity they would use.

QUESTION

What action do you think Lucy was going to suggest?

Lucy's environmental action was to use cool water whenever possible. She reasoned that she really didn't need hot water when she washed her hands. And she and Elliott washed their hands a lot! It's what helped keep the germs away and keep them healthy. Sure, it might be a little chilly, but it was only their hands. It wasn't like jumping into a cold bath or shower. Dad suggested that maybe they could just try washing hands in cool water in the summer when the cool water coming into the house wasn't so chilly. Mom also said that she was going to switch to the cold-water laundry soap.

MORE QUESTIONS

- Do you think your family could try Lucy's idea?
- What kind of system does your house use to heat up water for baths and showers?

It takes a lot of energy to wash our clothes, mostly just to heat the water. Only 10 to 15 percent of the energy used actually goes to running the washing machine.

Washing clothes in cold water will get your clothes just as clean as hot, except for maybe really stinky stuff like baby diapers, grease stains, or Dad's stinky gym clothes.

"Bills travel through the mail at twice the speed of checks."
STEVEN WRIGHT

20

Grow Your Own

Grandpa and Grandma were looking after Elliott and Lucy this weekend. The kids loved when their grandparents looked after them. There was always candy, cuddles, and stories. Elliott enjoyed the stories, Lucy loved the cuddles, and they both loved the candy. Today, Grandpa was telling stories about olden days when the whole world was in a war—twice! He wasn't talking about all of the nasty stuff, though. He was talking about gardens.

Grandpa said that during a big war before he was born, *his* mom told him that she had something called a "victory garden."

He and Grandma also had one during a second big war.

He explained what these gardens were all about. People who had yards were encouraged to grow a personal garden full of vegetables and herbs so others who had to buy food at stores would have enough.

"Sometimes food was hard to buy back then," Grandpa said. "So every little bit helped."

Grandma added, "And our fresh tomatoes were tastier than just about any I've ever had!"

Elliott asked, "You were growing organic vegetables way back then?"

Grandpa laughed, "Well, we didn't call it that then, but come to think of it, we didn't use any chemicals or bug sprays, and it was only the seeds and a little sweat and effort from us, so I guess . . . yes, sure, we had a little organic garden."

"Wow, talk about eating locally," Lucy exclaimed. "You can't get much more local than your very own backyard!"

Grandma said, "Every carrot or tomato you grow on your own is one that doesn't need a truck or a train to bring it to you. And as I said, they are sure tasty!"

Lucy understood this. "So it's good for us *and* the environment!" she said as she looked at a nice square patch of dirt in the backyard that used to be their sandbox.

Elliott looked too. It was as if they were thinking the same thing when they said in unison, "We have a great idea, Grandpa and Grandma!"

QUESTION

What do you think Elliott and Lucy's idea was?

Elliott and Lucy were going to suggest that they use their old sandbox area to plant a small vegetable garden. The kids were old enough now that they hardly ever played in the sandbox, so it was a perfect chance to *reuse* the area. There would be enough room to grow some tomatoes, beans, and carrots. Grandpa and Grandma suggested the beans and tomatoes because they grew on vines that grow upward and don't take too much room. They might even have enough room for some lettuce. Yum! Instant, home-grown, organic salad! Now, that's a real *green* action!

MORE QUESTIONS

◎ Have you ever grown vegetables?
◎ In the old days, they were called victory gardens. Can you explain why? Can you think of some fun modern names for a garden like Elliott and Lucy's?
◎ What is your favorite vegetable?

You don't need a yard to grow your own vegetables. Many vegetables, like tomatoes, can be grown on a balcony, a patio, even a windowsill. Small plants, like herbs, can fit almost anywhere.

Gardens are good for more than just food. A garden promotes good health and gives you some nice, gentle exercise, too.

> *"Weeds are flowers too, once you get to know them."*
> EEYORE

21

We'll Get New Wheels

It was early in the morning. Elliott, Lucy, and Mom were all seated at the dining table having breakfast. Dad kissed everyone good-bye and headed into the garage to get into the car and go to work. Within a minute, he was back with a very grumpy face and muttering those growly words under his breath that dads mutter when they're mad.

"What's the matter, honey?" Mom asked.

Dad grumbled, "Car. Not working. Again!"

As Dad dialed a taxi to get to work, he said, "That's the last straw—we're buying a new car. This week!"

Even though Mom loved their old car, she agreed it was time to get a new one.

"Yay!" Elliott and Lucy yelled. This sounded like fun!

That night at dinner, the whole family sat around the computer and looked at new cars. "This is probably a good time to make sure we get a car that doesn't hurt the environment too much," Mom said. Elliott and Lucy high-fived that idea.

"What kind of camper did Matt and Steph use to follow them around the country during their run, Elliott? It must have been a good one," Lucy asked. Elliott remembered that it was called a biodiesel RV. And that Steph said when she was running behind it, it smelled like French fries! Everyone laughed at that.

"Biodiesel is a nice idea, because the fuel comes from plants, but I don't think it's going to work out for our family," Dad said.

"We need a nice, economical vehicle that runs on fuels that we can get nearby," Mom added as she found a Web site for inexpensive new gas-powered cars. It was true they didn't use much gas, but Dad wanted to look at cars called "hybrids."

He clicked over to that section and explained that hybrids used electricity about half the time and went for a long distance on a tank of gas. He added that they didn't pollute at all when they were running on electricity.

Elliott spotted something else. "Look, Dad! This one is totally electric. No gas at all! You just plug it in at night to charge it up. Just like my video game!"

Dad's mouth curled into a smile. "Cool," he said. There certainly were a lot of choices in front of them.

QUESTION

Which kind of car would you like for your family?

There are so many things to think about when a family buys a car. How many seats do you need? Do you drive mostly in the city or on the highway? Does Mom like to feel "sporty" in the car she drives? Many eco-conscious families are buying hybrid cars and SUVs now. Electric cars are also a great choice because they don't pollute the air at all, and electricity is a renewable and sustainable resource. Unfortunately, there are not too many electric cars to choose from just yet, but they're coming.

MORE QUESTIONS

◎ What kind of fuel does your family car use?
◎ Why is it important to buy an efficient car?

Maybe a hybrid isn't right for your family, though. Some cars with a regular gas engine might not use too much fuel and won't pollute very much. Look for cars that are ULEV (ultra-low-emissions vehicles).

Some governments also provide tax incentives (free money) when you purchase a hybrid or electric vehicle.

> *"Your grandchildren will likely find it incredible—or even sinful—that you burned up a gallon of gasoline to fetch a pack of cigarettes!"*
> PAUL MACCREADY JR.

22

∽

To Light or Not to Light

Lucy loved to read. She would often take out a pile of books on the weekend and read each one of them, one right after another. She would read picture books, "how to" books, storybooks, and she had even begun reading short chapter books. It seemed as if she went from *The Little Red Hen* to *Julie's Young Lady Handbook* almost overnight. Yes, Lucy was getting to be a big girl.

Her love of books went back as far as she could remember, when Mom or Dad would sit down and read to her. She especially liked bedtime stories. But now, she often read in bed and on her own.

One night after lights out, Lucy sneaked a flashlight under the covers so she could keep reading. Mom peeked in from the hallway and knew exactly what was going on. She was secretly kind of happy that Lucy liked reading so much that she wanted to keep at it, but she still spoke in her sternest, firmest, Mom-means-business voice. "Lucy, you'll ruin your eyes using that flashlight. It's lights out. Now, young lady."

Lucy obeyed and said, "Okay, Mom. Nighty night!" Lucy clicked off the flashlight and smiled. Mom smiled, too.

After school the next day, Lucy decided to read in the playroom. She was staying indoors because it was a nasty, blustery, rainy day outside. That meant it was kind of dark inside with the drapes closed. The playroom was a little dark, but Lucy could still read just fine. That's when she remembered what Mom had said about reading at night with the flashlight. She didn't want to ruin her eyes! "Hmm," she thought as she looked at the light switch in the room. Then she looked up at the ceiling and re-membered that clicking on the switch in that room turned on one, two, three, four, five, six, seven, *eight* ceiling lights. She knew that clicking on the switch was way more light than she really needed. After all, it was just her and a book that needed light. "That would be a waste, I think." She pondered as her eyes focused on the chair beside the big window that had the drapes pulled back. She could see a little crack of outside light through the drapes and had a great idea. "I know how I can get enough light to read without using any energy!"

QUESTION

What energy-saving action was Lucy about to take?

Lucy realized that opening the drapes would give her enough light to read her book and not use one bit of energy, except for her own energy she would use to walk over and open them. Anytime you can make a decision not to use energy or electricity, it is a good decision. *Reduce* the amount of electricity you use. It's a great action!

MORE QUESTIONS

- When Lucy was about to click on the lights, how many bulbs would it have turned on? Why was it a good decision not to turn them on?
- Do you have a favorite place to read? Is it by a window for light?
- What is your favorite kind of book to read?

Natural light from the sun is free,
and it is the best lighting for reading.

*"If it weren't for electricity,
we'd all be watching television by candlelight."*
GEORGE GOBEL

23

Watch Your Water

One night, Elliott and Lucy were enjoying an indoor "camp-out" in the basement. They always enjoyed pretending to be sleeping outside all by themselves. Dad would set up the tent, and Mom always made sure that the sleeping bags were clean and the pillows were fluffed. Sure, it wasn't real camping, but it was fun to pretend.

After they zipped up the tent, Mom said, "See you in the morning!" and Dad added, "Watch out for wild animals!" Elliott and Lucy giggled for a while, then took turns gently trying to kick each other. Then they told stories about school, and then . . . well, then Lucy fell fast asleep. Elliott knew it was time to go to sleep, too, and he tried to drift off but just couldn't. He began to notice all the different sounds in the basement. The old clock in the corner that *tick, tick, ticked* away, the furnace that clicked on and off with a fan, and another noise that he couldn't quite recognize. It was a *drip-drip* sound, and it was nonstop. Every *drip-BONG* sounded like a drum being hit. *Drip-BONG!* He couldn't sleep. *Drip-BONG!* He still couldn't sleep. *Drip-BONG!* Elliott simply, just, could, not slee . . . SNNNNORE!

Eventually, Elliott fell asleep.

But the very next morning, as soon as he woke up, he searched around till he found the source of the sound. "Aha!" It was coming from the big laundry sink beside the washing machine. "Gotcha!" he said as he tried to tighten the tap. Unfortunately, that didn't stop the drip.

Mom entered the laundry room and said, "Oh, don't even try, Elliott. That hot-water tap has been leaking for ages. We have to get your dad to fix it, but he's not very motivated."

"Not motivated, huh?" Elliott said. That was all he needed. Elliott ran to the computer and opened the site he used when he was researching how much water was wasted when they used to leave the water running while the family brushed their teeth. He learned that a dripping tap like the one in the laundry sink can waste up to eight gallons of water every week. Just from one tiny drip! Elliott ran back downstairs to see Mom and proclaimed, "Mom, I think I know how we can get Dad to fix that drip . . . and do it tonight!" Mom was very curious about Elliott's plan.

QUESTION

What would Elliott do to get Dad to fix the tap?

Elliott appealed to his dad's sense of economy. In other words, he pointed out to Dad just how much money and hot water that one drip cost him every year. Dad was immediately motivated to bicycle down to the hardware store that weekend and buy the 25-cent washer that was needed to fix the drip. Mom winked at Elliott. Because of Elliott, she realized that the way to motivate Dad was not through reminders but through his wallet!

MORE QUESTIONS

⊚ Why is it good for the environment to stop a leaky faucet?
⊚ Why do you think Dad ignored the drip?
⊚ Do you have any drips in your house (no jokes, moms and dads!)?

Every faucet or showerhead that drips can cost
up to 15 to 20 dollars per year.

If you had three faucets and each one dripped once every second,
you would waste 8 gallons a day. That's 62 baths per year!

"All things are cheap to the saving, dear to the wasteful."
BENJAMIN FRANKLIN

*"I only feel angry when I see waste. When I see people
throwing away things that we could use."*
MOTHER TERESA

24

A Day at the Museum

Lucy loved to have fun and was always full of energy. Anytime there was a play to be acted in, a concert to be performed, or a dance to be danced, Lucy was first in line. She also liked painting and drawing. Dad said she was very creative.

One day, Lucy went on a school field trip to the museum. This place was full of all sorts of art. There were super-old paintings, statues that were made out of stone, and modern art, too. Lucy liked some of the old paintings, but a lot of them gave her the creeps, especially the ones of old people who looked as if they were staring right at her! Lucy mostly liked the modern art. The modern paintings she saw that day were full of bright colors and interesting shapes. In one part of the modern art section, her teacher showed her a room that was completely empty except for a chair. "This room is actually art, Lucy. It's called 'Sit,'" her teacher said.

Lucy replied, "That's weird." The next room was really interesting. It was filled with hundreds of what looked like puppets on sticks. Their heads were made out of pictures from magazines, books, and other odds and ends. The clothes were made out of bits of fabric, paper, and photos, too. Lucy's teacher explained that every puppet in the room was made out of something found. All of the materials used to make the puppets were reused from things that were made for some other purpose or recycled!

"Wow," said Lucy. "But I don't get it. What does having hundreds of weird-looking puppets in a room mean? Is that art?"

"Of course it is, Lucy," her teacher explained. "Sometimes art is only supposed to make you say 'Wow,' like you just did. Nothing more, nothing less. The art did its job." Lucy kind of liked that idea.

When she got home, Lucy was so inspired that she burst through the door. "I'm going to be an artist!" she exclaimed.

Mom and Dad always liked to encourage their kids to follow their dreams and immediately said, "Well, I guess we're going to need to buy you some paints and brushes!"

"Nope!" Lucy said. "I'm going to make environmentally friendly art. I learned about it at the museum," she said proudly.

Mom and Dad were very eager to hear what she had in mind and asked, "How?"

QUESTION

What was Lucy going to use to make her
environmentally friendly art?

Lucy decided to try being a "found art" artist. Her first project was something called a "collage," which was made out of old clippings and photographs from magazines and newspapers that were in the recycling bin. She also picked flowers and pressed them inside a large book until they dried and got tiny. Then she made them into beautiful little pictures. She got Dad to help her make frames for them out of one of Elliott's old hockey sticks. Lucy's action was to reuse things that were going to be thrown away and make them into something beautiful.

MORE QUESTIONS

◉ What did Lucy learn about the purpose of some art?
◉ Did Lucy like all of the art she saw at the museum?
◉ How is making art out of old things good for the environment?
◉ Can you think of some "found art" projects yourself?

The term *readymade art* was first used around 1915 and referred to art that was made out of old stuff. Snow shovels and bottle racks were used. In the 1980s, another name and style started, called Commodity Sculpture, and more recently, Trash Art or Junk Art has been used. You can imagine what that looks like.

"A great artist is always before his time or behind it."
GEORGE EDWARD MOORE

25

Too Cool for School

Elliott and Lucy's school was cool. They had two gyms, several art rooms, computer labs, and a great big cafeteria, too. The cafeteria also doubled as a cooking classroom, which both Elliott and Lucy enjoyed. They made all sorts of things, such as cupcakes, veggie dogs, pancakes, even ice cream.

One day, Elliott's cooking class decided to plan a fund-raiser, and one of the teachers thought it would be a great idea to sell homemade drinks. So, the kids would make lemonade because it was easy. After all, it was just lemon juice, sugar, and water. Elliott and his classmates really enjoyed slicing up the lemons and measuring out just the right amount of sugar for each jugful. Mr. Hatchingson, the school principal, was in charge of testing. The kids could tell from his puckered-up face whether it was too sour.

After each jug was made, it was Elliott's job to put the lemonade into the refrigerator. When he opened the fridge, he said, "Brrr! That is seriously cold in there." Then he happened to notice the temperature on the thermometer inside. It said 33 degrees. "Wow! No wonder it feels cold. That's nearly freezing!" Elliott said through his chattering teeth. That got him thinking. Just then the lunchtime bell rang.

After he had his lunch, Elliott went straight to the library and its Internet computer. He looked up "fridge temperatures" and found out that the best setting for a fridge is about 39 degrees. That's the right amount to keep food cold and not use too much energy. "Aha!" Elliott said, feeling like an energy detective. "I'm going to have a look around." With that, he ran around the school on a fridge hunt. He started to realize that the school was positively full of fridges. There were two in the staff room, a tiny one in Mr. Hatchingson's office, and four in the cafeteria. And every single one of them was set to the almost-freezing-your-face-off setting. Elliott knew exactly what he had to do. He marched up to Mr. Hatchingson and said, "Sir? I have a suggestion that will help save the school energy and money."

Mr. Hatchingson was all ears, accompanied by a big smile, as he listened to Elliott's plan.

QUESTION

What action do you think Elliott was about to suggest?

With Mr. Hatchingson's help, Elliott was allowed to go to every fridge in the whole school and turn the settings to the most efficient temperature. In total, they found fifteen fridges. (There was one in the science lab that they almost missed.) That was like helping every house on the block save energy, but it was all in just one school. Elliott felt pretty good about his idea, and so did Mr. Hatchingson. The principal mentioned Elliott's environmental action of saving fridge energy to the whole school at the next assembly. He even asked Elliott to stand up and take a bow!

MORE QUESTIONS

⊚ How did Elliott notice the temperature of the school fridges?
⊚ Where did Elliott learn about the best setting for fridges?
⊚ Why was it good that Elliott talked to the principal first?
⊚ Could you ask your parents to check the settings in your fridge?

Keep the cold air *in* your fridge. Open
the fridge only when you really need to.

Keeping that old fridge doesn't save you money. An average modern fridge sold today uses about one-third the amount of electricity compared with a fridge from 1973.

"The cheapest energy is the energy you don't use in the first place."
SHERYL CROW

26

❧

I Promise

It had been a year since Matt and Steph roared through town and Elliott and Lucy's school on their run around the continent to raise awareness of environmental issues. Their encouragement to the schoolkids to take action for the environment really got Elliott and Lucy thinking and acting throughout the year.

At dinner, Mom and Dad sat the kids down before they started eating. Dad opened the conversation and said, "You kids have been seriously earth-friendly this year."

Mom continued, "And you've really helped us grown-ups to pay attention to little habits, some bad ones, that could be really wasteful and not so nice for the environment."

Dad went on to say that he really felt that he and Mom had learned a lot from Elliott and Lucy. "You've really taught us some things and made us think," he said.

Elliott and Lucy high-fived each other. "That's what Matt said we should do!" Lucy said. "Yup, he said we should do what that song said and teach our parents well!"

Elliott jumped in to correct her "Matt-speak": "You mean well-*er*!" The whole family enjoyed a laugh.

Dad settled them down and said, "For the whole year, we've been keeping track of your actions, and Mom and I have something to show you."

Just then, Mom brought in a little tree made out of dried twigs with a wooden base. Elliott and Lucy hopped up and down. "What is it, what is it?"

Mom explained that it was a Promise Tree. "Every time one of you kids took an action, I wrote it down on a square of paper and hooked it on the Promise Tree," she said.

Elliott took a closer look and saw the cute little notes that said things like, "Turn Off Water," "Plant a Garden," "Recycle," and "Eat Locally." "This is totally cool!" Elliott said.

Lucy gave Mom and Dad a big hug. "You guys are the best," she said.

When she finally let go of Dad, he said, "It's called a Promise Tree for a reason. You have to keep those promises."

"We sure will!" Elliott and Lucy both agreed enthusiastically.

"Good," said Dad, "because there's more to this surprise, right, Mom?"

Mom nodded and motioned for everyone to come to the

window. She pointed into the backyard to a small evergreen tree. "That's our family's real Promise Tree. Dad and I planted it today," she said.

Dad reminded everyone that every time they saw the little tree, they should recall the promises or actions that they had accomplished this year. "And maybe we can add even more promises to the real tree. What do you think, family?"

Everyone cheered in agreement. They shared a group hug and knew that they would all try their very best to make decisions big and small to be good to our environment. Remember, every day is Earth Day!

Final Thoughts

"Oh Beautiful for smoggy skies, insecticided grain,
For strip-mined mountain's majesty above the asphalt plain.
America, America, man sheds his waste on thee,
And hides the pines with billboard signs, from sea to oily sea."
GEORGE CARLIN

"The universe is not required to be in perfect harmony
with human ambition."
CARL SAGAN

"People like to say we 'need to save the planet.' The planet
will be just fine. It will always find a way to adapt
and regenerate. It's humans and what we've built
that we're trying to save."
DAVID SUZUKI

Acknowledgments

To Sandra, my wife of twenty-seven years, and our spawn, Philip and Claire. You guys are the beginning, middle, and end of not only this book but all of my creative projects. XOXO

To Matt Hill and Stephanie Tait, who were crazy or, perhaps more appropriately, *brave* enough to take big-time action. Your run around our continent was truly an inspiration to me. Your positive spirit and passion for motivating kids to take environmental action is infectious. Keep going!

To David Milchard and Jason Bryden, who were the normal guys who showed me that there is a generation that really does ride bikes, save water, and recycle as a matter of course. Plus, they make me laugh.

To Ed Begley Jr., for "walking the walk" of being an environmentalist while at the same time avoiding being a militant, all the while doing so with incredible humor. You are a true inspiration.

I must also thank George Lucas. For *Star Wars,* Indiana Jones, and being my agent. Yes, folks, there are two George Lucases. The one I know is a pretty good dude.

A big thank-you to Greer Hendricks (my enthusiastic publisher and editor) and her son, Ethan (her "associate editor"), who worked on my first book, *E is for Ethics*, and also made this great little book happen. Thank you. You've made my transition into "authorin'" a supremely pleasant journey.

While we're on the subject of Ethan, thanks also to him and his pals at his school, St. Bernard's in New York. You were fabulous hosts. I hope all of my fans are as bright as you guys.

To my friend and the most versatile natural artist I know, Riley.

To Walt Disney for inspiring me to tell stories and imagine.

About the Author, Ian James Corlett

Ian James Corlett began telling stories at a very young age. He started with hand puppets and marionettes, which segued to a ventriloquist dummy, which leapfrogged into making animated films, then evolved into student comedy shorts, then led to creating and writing animated series and then writing this book.

Ian has written for and/or developed many popular children's series, such as *The Adventures of Paddington Bear, Will & Dewitt, Lunar Jim,* and *Rescue Heroes.* He has also created several original series, including his namesake show, *Being Ian.*

Ian is also a very well-known voice actor in the world of animation, entertainment, and advertising. He is the voice of literally hundreds of animated characters, including "The Conductor" on PBS's *Dinosaur Train,* "Dad" in *Johnny Test,* "Cheetor" of *Transformers/Beastwars* fame, and a dozen different characters, including "Mr. Pop" in *Dragontales.* He has been the TV promo voice of Family Channel, PBS, and Fox Kids, as well as commercial brands such as Best Buy, McDonald's, and Visa.

A father of two and husband of one for nearly thirty years, he enjoys hanging out with his kids, travel, and great food. He currently lives in Vancouver, Canada, and Palm Springs, California, where he and his family go to escape the drip and drizzle of the west coast of Canada.

Ian's one "vice," as he calls it, is a love of automobiles. He is most proud of his latest Porsche, a fully restored 1966. But this Porsche is a special one. Ian had it converted to 100 percent electric drive. With all of the classic looks on the outside but sporting ultramodern and environmentally friendly technology under the hood, it is Ian's pride and joy.

Ian's not-so-secret desire is to be a professional race-car driver, and he is quick to point out that Paul Newman started racing at forty-seven. For more about Ian, visit www.ianjamescorlett.com.

About the Illustrator

R. A. Holt is a Canadian-based illustrator, designer, and artist who resides in Vancouver, Canada.

Growing up in a small town on Vancouver Island, Riley spent his days outdoors catching frogs, bugs, and other creatures or by the sea, combing the beach for treasures. He had a fascination with intricate patterns and even the smallest details of the world around him. This study and rumination compelled him to create. Any objects Riley got hold of were quickly transformed into creatures and their accompanying worlds. Sometimes, to his parents' dismay, this involved Mom's dinner or Dad's brand-new tools. He began drawing and sculpting at a very young age and was driven to assimilate any style or technique he came across.

Although Riley had natural ability, he didn't consider himself an "artist." And so, upon completion of school, he decided to seek work in a trade, ultimately becoming a journeyman lithographer.

His spare time (and sometimes work time) was still spent in creative pursuits. He soon began using computers to create digital artwork and also turned his hand to making one-of-a-kind art toys. Despite the allure of rooms full of printing presses, ink and paper, he eventually made the decision to pursue art full-time.

Riley is self-taught, with no formal training in art. He has a wide range and uses many different mediums in his broad spectrum of artwork, examples of which can be seen at www.rileyholt.com.

Ian James Corlett knew of Riley's artwork and asked him to design Elliott and Lucy for his first book, *E is for Ethics*. Ian had exacting specifications: "Big heads! They must have big heads!" It was a perfect fit. Since then, Riley and Ian have worked on several books and creative projects, and Riley is the chief designer for the animated series based on Elliott and Lucy.

This is Riley's second book as an illustrator. He hopes you like his pictures!